ISBN: 978-1-85103-460-4

Originally published as *Franz Schubert Découverte des Musiciens* jointly by Editions Gallimard Jeunesse & Erato Disques

© & ℗ 1999 Editions Gallimard Jeunesse & Erato Disques

English text © & ℗ 2001 Moonlight Publishing Ltd & The Associated Board of the Royal Schools of Music

This edition was published in 2017 in the United Kingdom by Moonlight Publishing Ltd, 36 Milton Park, Abingdon, Oxfordshire, OX14 4RT

Printed in China

FRANZ
Schubert

FIRST DISCOVERY MUSIC

Written by Paule de Bouchet
Illustrated by Charlotte Voake
Narrated by Michael Cantwell

A house with a funny name 'At the Sign of the Red Crab' in Vienna is the birthplace of Franz Peter Schubert in 1797. His father, Franz Theodor, is a teacher and, like many people from Vienna, he loves music.

1 5TH SYMPHONY, 4TH MOVEMENT, ALLEGRO VIVACE
'MARCHE MILITAIRE' OP. 51 NO. 1, ALLEGRO VIVACE

In Vienna, music is everywhere: not just in concert halls, but also in the streets, the cafes, the gardens, the shops and at every kind of party.

When Franz is four his family moves from 'At the Sign of the Red Crab' to a house called the Black Horse.

WHAT IF...?

A country is known by its language, its climate, its music. Do you know how to play 'What if...?' You have to guess which country someone is thinking of by asking 'What if...?' What if it were a piece of music? It could be Bach, rock, rap or a dance...

Franz begins music lessons at the age of seven. His father teaches him the violin, as he had his two older sons, and Franz's oldest brother Ignaz teaches him the piano. After only a few months, he is already better than

2 PIANO TRIO NO. 2 IN E-FLAT MAJOR, OP. 100, 2ND MOVEMENT, ANDANTE CON MOTO

his father. He then takes lessons from a professional music teacher, Michael Holzer, who finds he has never had a pupil so musical. "I have nothing more to teach him."

MUSIC IS EVERYWHERE

A musician experiences the world through sound. Try a test: see if you can identify every sound you hear – a car, a vacuum cleaner, the sound of the wind, a piece of music you like...

When Franz is eleven, he sings in his church choir, plays the violin exceptionally well and is already writing little pieces for string quartet and for the piano.

3 CANTATA IN HONOUR OF JOSEF SPENDOU, 'WEH EUCH KINDERN, WEH EUCH ARMEN'

His father is proud of him and enters him for a scholarship to the Imperial Chapel choir. In his fine blue suit, Franz is by far the best, is congratulated by the jury, and wins a place at the best college in Vienna.

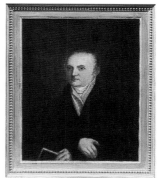

Schubert's father

LIKE A CONCERT !

Have you ever sung to an accompaniment? If you have no-one to accompany you, on the piano or the guitar for example, just find the tape or CD of a song and try singing along with it as in karaoke. You'll see, it feels great!

A new life begins. Franz has left his family and become a boarder, but it is not always fun. The college surroundings are drab and the food is not terribly good. Franz would love a few treats...

FEELINGS IN MUSIC

When you like a piece of music, it is often because it expresses emotions that you feel too: happiness, anger, wanting to cry... Listen to your favourite pieces and try to describe which feelings they arouse in you.

4 'MOMENT MUSICAL' OP. 94, NO. 3
ALLEGRO MODERATO

But what is most important to him is music. He also discovers friendship at the college. He spends hours explaining to his new friend, Joseph, how he tries to translate his thoughts into music.

During the holidays, when Franz comes home, the family makes music together: father plays the cello, brother Ferdinand the first violin, brother Ignaz the second violin and Franz always plays the viola part. When his

PICK OUT THE SOUNDS

Can you identify the sounds of different instruments when they are played together? In this quartet, try to pick out the deep sound of the cello, the middle range of the viola and the high pitch of the violins.

5 QUARTETTSATZ, [QUARTET PIECE]
ALLEGRO ASSAI

father makes a mistake, Franz points it out gently: 'Father dear, there seems to be a wrong note here.' At fourteen, Franz is composing lots of music for the 'Schubert Quartet'.

Franz is fifteen and can think of nothing but composing – piano pieces, string quartets, songs and even a symphony. He writes so much music so quickly that he quite often runs out of music paper. As he has no money to

16

Schubert finished writing the musical score of 'The Trout' in 1817, one Monday evening at midnight. He noted, 'Half asleep, I picked up the inkpot and spilt it over the score. What a disaster!'

buy more, he has to trace the lines himself on ordinary paper. All this takes much more time than his school work, and his father is furious!

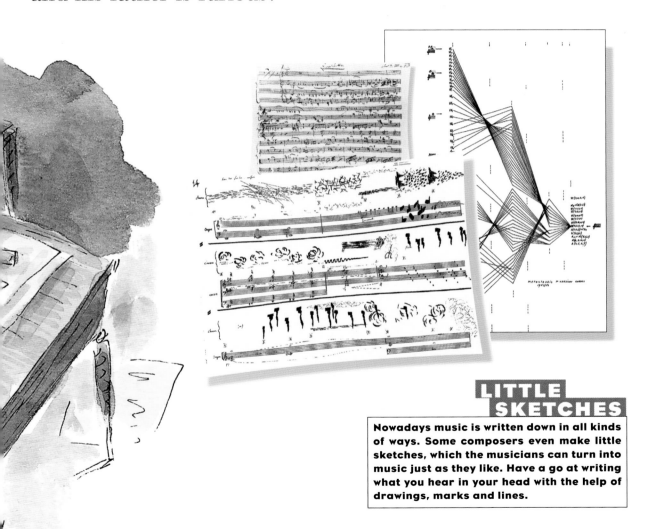

LITTLE SKETCHES

Nowadays music is written down in all kinds of ways. Some composers even make little sketches, which the musicians can turn into music just as they like. Have a go at writing what you hear in your head with the help of drawings, marks and lines.

One autumn day, Franz's first mass is being performed. Therese, the little soprano, sings so well that he falls in love with her. A few days later he composes a tragic song to the words: 'My peace of mind is gone, my heart is heavy-laden.' He is seventeen and senses that happiness will never be his. Franz falls ill at the age of twenty-five and dies at the age of thirty-one, leaving behind one of the finest and most wonderful collections of compositions.

A TRUE ROMANTIC

Schubert was a true romantic artist, who drew his inspiration from painful experiences and his deepest feelings. Have you noticed that when you are sad, you often want to be alone to read, write, paint or listen to music?

7 MASS NO. 6 IN E-FLAT MAJOR, AGNUS DEI

Today,

as in the past,

Schubert's

music

is played

and loved.

THE TROUT

The 'lied' is a simple song for voice and piano and is at the heart of Schubert's music. Schubert wrote over six hundred songs, or lieder. inspired by poetry. Like rainbows with their many shades of colour, poems are coloured by the many shades of our feelings. *Gretchen at the Spinning-wheel*, for example, is a poem of despair – a girl has been abandoned by the man she loves, and she is driven mad by the pain. In *The Trout*, by contrast, we are by the water's edge, the river is sparkling in the sunlight, and we see flashes of the leaping trout in the stream.

Lieder can be sung by female or by male voices.

Singing lieder is very different from singing opera: some singers have specialised in lieder.

20

'ARPEGGIONE'

Schubert's public was composed of those closest to him. It was for them, his family and friends, that he composed, and whom he joined in fun evenings, where his songs were sung and his chamber music was played. They loved to get together to dance and to drink beer! These social evenings, steeped in Schubert's music, were called 'Schubertiades' by his friends. For some musicians, tunes are less important than tone, rhythm or harmony, but for Schubert tunes were all-important. He occasionally found inspiration for his tunes in the most unexpected everyday sounds, for example, certain motifs in the following quartet came to him one day when he heard the grinding of an old coffee mill!

22

Schubert wrote fifteen string quartets including 'Death and the Maiden' in which feelings are expressed with some intensity.

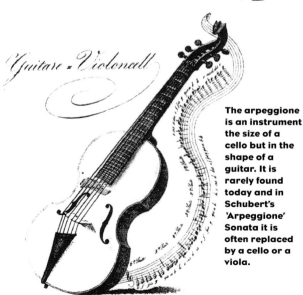

The arpeggione is an instrument the size of a cello but in the shape of a guitar. It is rarely found today and in Schubert's 'Arpeggione' Sonata it is often replaced by a cello or a viola.

MUSICAL MOMENTS

Schubert wrote a lot of music for the piano. The piano, with its singing tone, was his favourite instrument, and he constantly returned to it throughout his life.

He composed marvellous, deep soulful sonatas; he wrote dozens of dances, called 'ecossaises' (Scottish), 'deutsche' (German), 'polonaises' (Polish), 'galops', waltzes and minuets. Then there were variations, divertissements, fantasies and impromptus. He also wrote many piano duets ('for four hands'). Some pieces, which he called 'musical moments', have truly become some of the great moments of music.

Schubert composed his works on the pianos of the period.

He could scarcely have imagined the infinitely greater and richer sound that the modern concert piano would bring to his pieces.

24

SONATA IN A MAJOR D. 959, 2ND MOVEMENT, ANDANTINO
IMPROMPTU, OP. 90, NO. 2 ALLEGRO; 'MOMENT MUSICAL', OP. 94, NO. 4, MODERATO

THE 'UNFINISHED' SYMPHONY

Schubert was nineteen when he composed his fifth symphony. Just listen to the vivacity, the strength and the energy of this symphony, written by a still very young Schubert, who seems to be brimming over with *joie de vivre*. Some years later he wrote a symphony, known as the 'Unfinished' which portrayed his deepest feelings in music. He said through this music what he also wrote in a letter to a friend: 'I would celebrate love, but what I express instead is pain.' Schubert's music is a mixture of life's joy and despair, of song and sadness, of friendship and loneliness. It mirrors Schubert himself: a great nature-lover, yet shut in his room, surrounded by friends, and yet so alone, sometimes joyful but so often deeply unhappy.

26

Schubert's music reflects all that made up his life – indeed all that is in life as we experience it, just as music should do.

Schubert's 'Great' C Major Symphony begins with a long summons played by the French horns.

MOONLIGHT PUBLISHING

Translator
Penelope Stanley-Baker

ABRSM (PUBLISHING) LTD

Project manager:
Leslie East

English narration recording:
Ken Blair of BMP Recording

ERATO DISQUES

Artistic and Production Director:
Ysabelle Van Wersch-Cot

LIST OF ILLUSTRATIONS

PHOTOGRAPHIC ACKNOWLEDGEMENTS

Archiv für Kunst und Geschichte, Paris **8**, **8-9**, **11**, **12**, **13**, **14l**, **19**, **20b**, **22t**, **23**, **25**, **26t**, **27**. Artothek **21**. Collection Viollet **16**. Ph. Coqueux/Specto **20m**, **22m**, **24t**. G. Dagli Orti **7**. D.R. **17tl**, **17r**, **22b**, **26m**. Mary Evans/Explorer **18**, **20t**. Nicolas Frize **17bl**. Constantine Manos/Magnum **26b**. Pierre-Marie Valat **14r**, **24b**.

CD

I. House 'At the Sign of the Red Crab'
5th Symphony;
4th movement, Allegro vivace
The Netherlands Radio Chamber
Orchestra
Conducted by Ton Koopman
0630 15518 2
℗ Erato Disques SAS, Paris,
France 1997

'Marche militaire', Op. 51 No. 1,
Allegro vivace
Maria-Joao Pires and Hüseyin Sermet
(piano 4 hands)
0630 10718 2
℗ Erato Classics SNC, Paris,
France 1989

2. Better than his father
Piano Trio No. 2 in E-flat major, Op. 100,
2nd movement, Andante con moto
Haydn-Trio, Vienna
Heinz Medjimorec, piano
Michael Schnitzler, violin
Walter Schulz, cello
0630 12337 2
℗ Teldec Classics International, GmbH,
Hamburg, Germany 1987

3. A fine blue suit
Cantata in honour of Josef Spendou,
'Weh euch Kindern, weh euch Armen'
Ruth Ziesak, soprano
Wiener Concert-Verein
Arnold Schoenberg Choir
Conducted by Erwin Ortner
℗ Teldec Classics International, GmbH,
Hamburg, Germany 1994

4. Music above all else
'Moment musical', Op. 94 No. 3,
Allegro moderato
Till Fellner, piano
0630 17869 2
℗ Erato Disques SAS, Paris,
France 1997

5. The 'Schubert Quartet'
Quartettsatz [Quartet piece],
Allegro assai

Quartet Sine Nomine
Patrick Genet, François Gottraux,
violins; Nicolas Pache, viola
Marc Jaermann, cello
Cascavelle, 1987

6. A passion for composing
5th Symphony;
2nd movement, Andante
The Netherlands Radio Chamber
Orchestra
Conducted by Ton Koopman
0630 15518 2
℗ Erato Disques SAS, Paris,
France 1997

7. I've lost my peace of mind
Mass No. 6 in E-flat major,
Agnus Dei
Choeur de Chambre Romand
Choeur Pro Arte de Lausanne
Choirmaster, André Charlet
Orchestre de la Suisse romande
Conducted by Armin Jordan
Cascavelle 1988
Coproduction Erato/Cascavelle/RTSR
℗ Cascavelle

8. The songs
Gretchen at the Spinning-wheel
The Trout
Barbara Bonney, soprano
Geoffrey Parsons, piano
4509 90873 2
℗ Teldec Classics International, GmbH,
Hamburg, Germany 1994

9. Chamber music
'Arpeggione' Sonata, 1st movement
Frédéric Lodéon, cello
Daria Hovora, piano
℗ Erato Classics SNC,
Paris, France 1983

String Quartet 'Death and the Maiden',
1st movement, Allegro
Quartet Keller
Andras Keller, Janos Pilz, violins
Zoltan Gal, viola
Otto Kertesz, cello

4509 99780 2
℗ Erato Disques SAS, Paris,
France 1995

10. Piano music
Sonata in A major, D. 959,
2nd movement, Andantino
Michel Dalberto, piano
0630 14442 2
℗ Erato Classics SNC, Paris,
France 1985

Impromptu, Op. 90 No. 2, Allegro
Maria Joao Pires, piano
0630 10716 2
℗ Erato Classics SNC, Paris,
France 1988

'Moment musical', Op. 94 No. 4,
Moderato
Till Fellner, piano
0630 17869 2
℗ Erato Disques SAS, Paris,
France 1997

II. The Symphonies
5th Symphony;
1st movement, Allegro
The Netherlands Radio Chamber
Orchestra
Conducted by Ton Koopman
0630 15518 2
℗ Erato Disques SAS, Paris,
France 1997

8th Symphony 'Unfinished',
1st movement, Allegro moderato
Basel Symphony Orchestra
Conducted by Armin Jordan
0630 11081 2
℗ Erato Classics SNC,
Paris, France 1983

'Great' C Major Symphony;
3rd movement, Scherzo, Allegro vivace
New Philharmonia Orchestra
Conducted by Theodor Guschlbauer
0630 11081 2
℗ Erato Classics SNC, Paris,
France 1972

FIRST DISCOVERY MUSIC

JOHANN SEBASTIAN BACH
LUDWIG VAN BEETHOVEN
HECTOR BERLIOZ
FRYDERYK CHOPIN
CLAUDE DEBUSSY
GEORGE FRIDERIC HANDEL
WOLFGANG AMADEUS MOZART
HENRY PURCELL
FRANZ SCHUBERT
PYOTR ILYICH TCHAIKOVSKY
ANTONIO VIVALDI

LOUIS ARMSTRONG
RAY CHARLES
ELLA FITZGERALD